# **POETIC PRAISE**

## CHRISTIAN POETRY BY MARGARET SUSAN WALKER

## ALL GLORY FOR ALL THINGS BE TO GOD ALMIGHTY!!

*Praise God!*
*Margaret Walker*

# Poetic Praise

| | | | |
|---|---|---|---|
| GODS LOVE | 5 | I WANT TO HEAR YOU SING | 95 |
| THE HONEYSUCKLE | 11 | BORN TO FLY | 99 |
| MY SISTER | 15 | Dances on the Wind | 105 |
| I AM WORTHY | 21 | DO AS I ASK-THE VICTORY OF CONFESSION | 107 |
| DOUBTERS PRISON | 27 | BLOOM WHERE YOU GROW | 109 |
| MY MIRROR | 31 | WHO IS GOING TO HEAVEN | 113 |
| SILENCE | 33 | PASTOR LEROY | 119 |
| TO HIS KNEES | 35 | I SURRENDERED- HE ANSWERED | 125 |
| THE GIFT | 43 | PAINTING OUTSIDE OF THE LINES | 127 |
| WHAT WAS IT ALL FOR | 51 | MY LOVE | 129 |
| LISTEN TO ME CHILDREN | 55 | PAID IN FULL | 131 |
| I GIVE UP | 57 | DAD | 133 |
| I KNOW YOU GIRL | 65 | PRAISING THROUGH | 136 |
| HEALER BE THY NAME | 69 | MEREDITH(BABY GIRL) WALKER | 140 |
| MY SHEPHERDS CANE | 73 | MADAILEIN(KIKI) WALKER | 142 |
| MARTINSVILLE ON SOLID GROUND | 77 | JOY IN CLASS | 147 |
| THANKSGIVING FEAST | 81 | OUT IN FAITH | 153 |
| KEEP HIM | 87 | THERE IS NO END WITH JESUS | 157 |

[3]

[4]

I think that the most amazing thing about joining Gods family was that the transformation was so automatic. I had to believe, I had to surrender my fears and my heart to God but the rest came to pass all on its own. The speed at which your life changes depends on your willingness to give control of your life to God. Some longtime Christians are still holding on to their power and asking why they are not as fulfilled as others. It is like jumping from a building at first. Some find faith and jump with both feet. Some try to figure out how to scale down slowly. Others stand at the top for a very long time, study the situation, and then jump all at once when no one expects it. Those are GREAT moments! All ways are fine as long as the goal is the same. We are all in this together. First searching, then learning, then accepting, and finally praising. So many people say to me" I don't have to be in church to be saved. I don't need to worship or spend time with other believers to be a part of the kingdom of Heaven." The thing that I say to them is that when you are brought into the family of God your desires to be with other worshipers and to praise His name out loud increase. Church and the church family are a bi-product of the most beautiful birth in your life, the birth of your spirit into Christ. Everything is new, everything is wonderful. The color green is greener. The smell of honeysuckle is sweeter and the feel of the sun is somehow warmer. The memories of yesterday are somehow quieted by the promise of tomorrow.

 GODS LOVE

When I think of God's love, I think of family

When I think of God's love, I think of friends

When   I think of God's love, I think of the Bible

When it comes to God's love there's no end

I think of the rain that washes us

I think of the sun that dries

I think of the plants that feed us

I think of what pleases our eyes


I think of the mountains we climb on

I think of the rivers we swim

I think of the mattress I lay on

And the prayers that I offer to him


All of the grandest of places

All of the smallest of things

All are a subject of praises

When I think of what God's love means


But the greatest of all of these gifts

The one that I cherish the most

Is the love God placed in my heart

That He allows me to host

I feed it each day with the bible

I exercise using its glow

I share it with all of the world

Even those who don't want to know

I weed it on a regular basis

So that hatred cannot take root

I trim it and keep it in comfort

My hope is that it will bear fruit

I can give you a start if you want one

You don't have to prequalify

But you must learn the proper care

So that you won't cause it to die

AND THEN

When you think of God's love, You will KNOW family

AND

When you think of God's love, You will KNOW friends

AND

When you think of God's love, You will KNOW the Bible

AND

And ALL of the power within………..


Praise God!!

[9]

[10]

The honeysuckle is one of my favorite flowers. It looks very sweet and the flowers are quite tiny. It grows from within and weaves together so tightly that when the summer is over it is very hard to cut the plant down. The smell of this flower is unmistakable. Such a heavy and sweet smell. You can find the aroma on a warm summer breeze carried from far away. When our church is strong and we hold each other up in celebrations and in tragedies, we are like the honeysuckle. When we bond together in praise you can smell the aroma of victory from far away.

## THE HONEYSUCKLE

Because the honeysuckle smells so sweet
Lest I never forget
The perfume of Heaven is what I smell
And I stand in awe of the debt.

The seed drops to the ground
Dried and broken in
Nothing but a shell
Forgotten in the wind.

The pain of leaving the root
The pain of falling so far
The uncertainty of having no strength
Yet being cast out into this war

Because the honeysuckle smells so sweet
Lest I never forget

The perfume of Heaven is what I smell
And I stand in awe of the debt

And in the darkness some movement
A stem begins to unfold
The pushing away of the shell
The hardships still untold

The stem breaking through the shell
Still must root in the ground
Still must find a solid place
To anchor its foundation down

The water, the sun, the soil
They will all be needed here
The nutrients of Gods awesome promise
Will lift away the fear

Up and up, it sees the sun
It grows up full and strong
The seed is but a memory
The darkness is all gone

Its power is awesome and mighty
Its size is hearty and great
It grows in spite of the doubt now
Its purpose in life to create

Because the honeysuckle smells so sweet
Lest I never forget
The perfume of Heaven is what I smell
And I stand in awe of the debt.


The weather is growing cold now
The honeysuckle weeps.
Its fruit will soon be dropping
It will have to release its seeds

Alas it will start again.
With nothing but a shell
That must be broken apart
For God to fill its well

Lord I know that you don't need me
To change this course of life
I am just honored to smell the beauty
That you bring from all the strife

Because the honeysuckle smells so sweet
Lest I never forget
The perfume of Heaven is what I smell
And I stand in awe of the debt.

I will NEVER, NEVER forget……Praise God!

[14]

The strongest bonds that we make in the church are often a bi product of our service to God. The choir, the mission trips, the church board, church musicals. Times spent in fellowship while serving God in some way can build friendships that last a lifetime. Many times you affect someone around you without even knowing that you have given them blessings. The great thing about Gods family is that those little silent blessings often come back to you in Gods time, at the precise moment that you need them. This poem is one of my very favorites because there have been many "Sister Mary's" in my life.

## My Sister

Sister Ruby lies in pain
The hospital numbered her days
Cancer has taken her physical strength
This is her final phase

She has made a peace of it
And she is glad to go
She can't wait to see the Lord
And leave behind her woes

Her pain is very high
The doctors do their best
But even with medication

She can barely rest.

Sister Mary comes in
They go to the same church
She never speaks a word
She sits down with her purse

She starts to sing the gospel
She sings it loud and clear
She sings and sings for hours
Night is drawing near

Ruby stopped her sister
With tears upon her face
Mary turned to listen
Smiling full of Grace

As you sang I saw my Mother
Cleaning up the house
And lifting up the Lord in song
Like angels from her mouth

As you sang I saw my Dad
Watching Mom with pride
As she sang in the choir box
And we sat by his side

And as you sang I saw my child

A newborn in her crib
I sang to her to let her rest
And that is what she did

My pain it seems so distant now
My joy is just so strong
I cannot wait for heaven
I hope it isn't long

Sister how did you know
That would cause my pain to end

Mary said:
Because I am your sister
Where you stop, I begin

I don't know why you were chosen
To enter the pearly gates.
But I know that our God is wise
So we should celebrate

And I know that as your sister
Some of our strongest bonds
Came through the hymns at church
Worshiping through song

We sang through our triumphs
We sang through our pain

We sang through our victories
We sang through the rain

So sister it is only fitting
That I sing to you right now
I'm going to sing you into heaven
As surely you are bound


And sister I am sure
That when your life does end
I will be in the front of the church
Singing hymns for you again

I hold you up to God
My precious loving friend
And ask that you keep singing
Until we meet again

Ruby said:

My sister I must tell you
Your love has blessed my soul
And when I get to heaven
I will let our Father know

I leave behind great memories
And friendships in this place

But I take with me my strength
And my Victory and my Grace


Then Ruby just laid back,
And didn't make a sound
And then drifted off to sleep

And then was heaven bound

Praise God and be your sisters' keeper!

[20]

My discipleship teacher brought an article in one day and asked me to read it. "This has always meant a lot to me and I wondered if you could make a poem out of it" he said. I kept it for several days and nothing came. One night on my way home from work, I was listening to a preacher on the radio. Her whole message was about self worth and how we fail to see the beauty in ourselves. Her message sparked something in me and all of a sudden I was pulling into the gas station and writing on the back of a paper bag that I found in the floor. The poem below was born that day. I got home and typed it out and looked up the radio preacher and sent her a copy in email to which she never responded. I took a copy to my Sunday school class the following week and it was a wonderful class full of victory. God is always in love with us. The negative forces that we carry in our heart are not from God.

## I AM WORTHY

A thought was in my head today
I could not seem to shake
It made me feel unworthy
Of God in heavens wake

I remember when I had the chance
To hold the lord up high
Sometimes I took the low road
And put up little fight

Many years have passed
And many times I fell
My thoughtless transgressions
I remember all to well

Lord I know you see me
And you know that I'm alone

I come to you on bended knee
And bow down at your throne

I am saddened by my progress
I am not who I should be
I look out on your works of life
And the least of all is me

I grabbed my things to leave
A dollar hit the floor
I reached to pick it up
And then headed for the door

I finally arrived at work
And stepped out of the car
That dollar fell again
But this time it went far

It blew across the wind
Right down into the muck
Then got flattened to the road
By the tires of a truck

I reached to pick it up
That nasty dirty bill
And shook away the mud
And held it closer still

In the door at work
I put my dollar in my tray
It must have looked like trash

For it was quickly thrown away

So then I had to fish
Through everybody's mess
To find my dirty dollar
And retrieve it to my desk

Sitting there alone
I slumped into my chair
Today had barely started
And I was feeling such despair

That is when I saw the Lord
He sat down next to me
"Do not cry my child" He said
"Tell me what it is you seek"

I cried out to my Lord
I am nothing and no one
I am tarnished and bruised
Of worth I have none.

How can I be worthy
Scarred from all my sin
If I knocked on heaven's door
Would you really let me in

How can I compare
To the saints that walk your ground
How could I expect
That my soul is heaven bound

The lord took my hand
And He smiled a knowing smile
"Now rest your fear my little one
And YOU listen for awhile

When you dropped your money
And it crumpled on the floor
Did you want it any less
than you wanted it before

When your money blew
Into mud and made a mess
Did the dirt and soil that covered it
Make you want it any less

And when it was discarded
Casually thrown away
Did you say good riddance
And walk the other way

You knew that dollar had worth
And you followed it to the end
The dirt did not diminish
The value from within

Now look into my heart
For that is what I see
When life is beating you down
And pushing you from me

I do not see the bruises
I do not see the dirt
I see your inner value
And you're endless worth

Do not ever doubt me child
I forgave you of all of your sin
And I relish in your beauty
That comes from deep within

Thank you Oh My God
You have given such a peace
My questions have been answered
And I feel a huge relief

The devil tried to trick me
He told me that I am a fool
He told me I was worthless
And unworthy of your rule

But my Father I had forgotten
That Your son DIED for me
Because You KNEW my worth
And You CHOSE to set me free…………PRAISE GOD!!!!

As in all things, the very beginning of your Christian walk can be so beautiful and so promising. Then we start to try to pick apart the promise to see if it will really hold up to the weather. This next poem was written in just such a time. The pain may not go away for a very long time but the key is to remain faithful and the pain will go away.

## DOUBTERS PRISON

Lord my steps seem labored now
The newness has worn off
The trumpets that were sounding near
Do play a little rough

The sunrise came as yesterday
I made it to my feet
Though all is lost in questions
And feeling some defeat

I hold my breath this moment
And chase the doubts away
I scream out, "Halleluiah"
I hope the mood won't stay

You are all that I have
My debt which you have paid
My only hope to salvation
Through weak and dangerous days

I can see where the lost fall back deeper
As their misery unfolds
Who can they ask for assistance
When there warm blood turns cold

Who will reach out to hold them
Who will cradle their head
Who will show them their worth when
They think that their better off dead

The world wants to claim their possessions
The world wants to burn up their joy
Who'll teach them how to fight for it
While they're battered around like a toy

And when they're exhausted from battle
Who will understand
Will they even know what they're fighting for
Amongst the worldly men

I come to You exhausted Lord
I cannot see the prize
You hold my hand and walk me through
You show me what is wise

I hold my breath this moment
And chase the doubts away
I scream out, "Halleluiah"

I hope the mood won't stay

I trust You God eternal
I know that You are true
My mood is just a reflection
Of the Devil getting through

I will work to chase him out
And free my heart again
So the blessing that I need so much
Has room to come in

And once again I see Oh Lord
That one forgotten praise
Can leave me with a worldly view
To fight for all my days

Praise God! All of the time!

[30]

I grew up as a fat little girl.  I learned very early on how to criticize that young lady in my mirror.  My constant criticisms caused pain and hopelessness deep within me.  What God restored to me was the right to love myself.  God showed me that it was His desire for me to be loved at all stages in my life and at all stages in my Christianity.

<u>My Mirror</u>

I used to look in the mirror
At my misery unseen
A reflection of worldly greed
staring back at me.

I thought that I could change my hair
Or maybe lose some weight
I thought that if I'd buy some clothes
Then love would end the hate

I did all that and much much more
and nothing seemed to work
I could not reach that peaceful place
My misery still did lurk

Then one day in desperation

I let the Lord come in
I opened up my heart and soul
And allowed His work to begin

He cleaned up all of my secret spots
Where disgust and depression hid
He took away my hopelessness
He opened up the lid

The light just poured all down my life
and washed away my sin
And now when I look in the mirror
I just see a beautiful grin

PRAISE GOD!!

[32]

We all go through horrible things. God does not cause them to happen. He only gives us the strength to hold on through them. In the midst of my tragedy I found the two most important things for me to do were to keep silent enough to hear Gods direction and to hold Gods hand through the battle.

## Silence

My feet move but by faith now Lord
My security is gone
My path that I thought was set in stone
Now breaks a brand new dawn

For just a fleeting moment
I sounded out of fear
And cast the darts of anguish
Not regarding who may hear

But silence falls upon me Lord
As I lay this at Your feet
I sit and listen intently
No surrender, no defeat

This battle has begun Lord
But I fight without a voice
Through my prayers and meditation
I am able to rejoice

My Lord I trust You fully
And I move down to my knees
Let my silence show my faith Lord
Let my prayers serve to please

Put me back in check Lord
I need not know the plan
Please hold me in my weakness
Cradle my family in your hands

Praise God!!

[34]

There is a time and a moment for most all Christians in which we realize that as much as we thought we were in control, we really are not.  Those times start off being the worst times in our lives until we lay the problems at the feet of the Lord.  Suddenly, our worst days become the birth of our best days.

## TO HIS KNEES

And as children we laughed and played

Because we knew the time had come

Tomorrow was the day

Anticipation of lots of fun

The tree was glistening brightly

The hallways smelled like spice

The windows were smudged rightly

While checking for reindeer in flight

And Grandma yelled from the kitchen

Who broke my little doll

We all ran to hide

Leaving Devin to take the fall


Grandpa called out for us

It is time to tell a tale

Popcorn balls and hot cocoa

And for the grownups Ginger ale


Grandpa started to talk

Such a big bear of a man

"I am not going to tell you about Santa

Tonight"

You already know of his plans


I am going to tell you about Jesus

And a tear ran down his cheek

I remember my mouth flying open

Watching grandpa try to speak

There was a time that I did not know

Who baby Jesus was

Your Grandma tried to tell me

She showed me with her love


I thought that it was a story

Passed down from age to age

A nice and helpful story

But best left for the stage


Until I met with Him personally

One cold December night

I was driving all of us home

The car veered off to the right


We went down over a hill

And landed in the creek

I could not find your mother

And Grandma was very weak

With all that I had ever been

And all that I'll ever be

I knew that I could not fix this mess

This could not be changed by me

All at once I heard the voice

With Grandmas weakest breath

She was thanking God for all that she has

And promising faith with what was left

I managed to get out of the car

And looked around the grounds

There I saw your mother

She was in the snow face down

My life just went before my eyes

A lump was in my throat

I ran to her and scooped her up

I wrapped her in my coat

Back in the car I rocked and cried

And called the Lord by name

Grandma prayed as best she could

And then some helpers came

They went to the hospital right away

But I stayed there all night

It was my first time knowing my Lord and Savior

And I had to make things right

I realized on bended knee

The gift that God gave all

My child was limp from an accident

His child was chosen to fall

Then Grandpa smiled and wiped his tears

And looked at us, each one

Your choice is yours to make in life

The devil or the Son


He danced around the Christmas tree

And thanked God for our health

He thanked him for the gifts and food

And for our spiritual wealth


Grandma came from the kitchen

With a twinkle in her eye

Yes, she said, dear children

 Then she let out a big sigh


The Lord took hold of the wheel that night

And drove us to the place

Where Grandpas heart could be made right

To understand His grace

The only gift that I remember

From that wonderful Christmas eve

Was your Grandpa being born

Into Gods family

And every day since

Our souls are living free

Because Jesus Steered Grandpa in the right direction

And brought him to his knees

Praise God!

[42]

I ask myself again and again how Jesus could endure the pain, as a gift to all of the sinners left here on earth, knowing full well that He would not ever breathe in life again to see the outcome of His gift to mankind. That is faith at its highest.

## The Gift

Lord I ask Your company today

I have a question for You

I have pondered all that I can read

And I am not sure what to do

They say that You gave Your son for

me

Two thousand years ago

He paid the price of life for me

In order to save my soul

I did not know about Him Lord

I lived with all of my chains

I held them all up by myself

Until just a shell remained

And then a disciple of Yours

revealed Your gift to me

And it felt like my load got lighter Lord

I felt the chains release


I think that I understand Lord

The sacrifice You made

But I just can't wrap around

The reason that Jesus stayed


He knew that they would cause His death

He knew that it was time

He never tried to run away

He stayed for bread and wine

And when the pain was at its worst

And He knew this was the end

He asked for You to forgive us

To wipe away our sin


I Try to fathom the notion

of someone killing me

And my only thought

to pray for them

And ask that they be set free


And I just can't find a way Lord

To understand his ways

The courage that it took Lord

To surrender life in Praise

I heard a soft voice hearken

"I am glad to have you home"

We had a place held open here

Since the day that you were born

I appreciate your questions

And the best that I can say

The answers are not simple

And they won't all come today


The pursuit of that very truth

Will draw you down the road

And will help to shape your actions

And help you to be bold


Each struggle that you go through

Will bring another truth

Until I call you home to stay

Then the answers will live in you


My gift was the beginning

For each and every soul

The end is yet to be written

By the seeds you choose to sew


Understand that My love for you

Is the reason for it all

The desire of a father

Not to see his children fall


And as your path unfolds

And you feel the pain from life

React to save your brother

Don't surrender or take flight

Lead your people back

Back to where it all began

When My Son laid down his life for all

And died with outstretched hands


Be glad this year as Christmas comes

You were chosen to be free

Accept your gift with open arms

And choose eternity


Praise God!!!

[49]

[50]

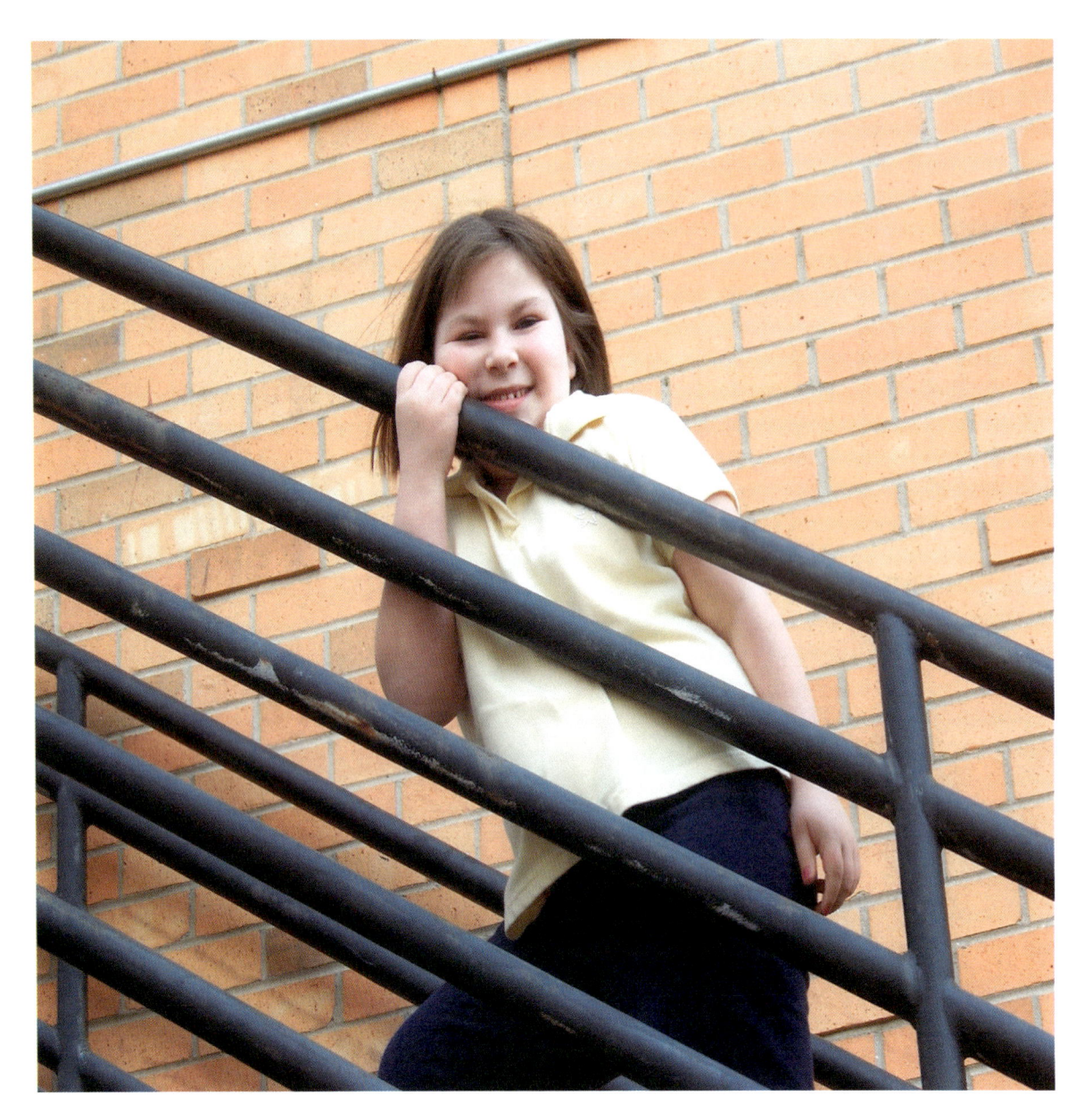

This next poem was a request from a preacher. He had left the pulpit and is now traveling in a musical quartet. His voice is very blessed and touches many hearts. He said to me one night after a concert that he would love to have a poem that captures the power of the pulpit. Most people don't understand what it really is all about. Until I started trying to write the poem, I don't think that I ever really gave it a second thought myself.

## What was it all for?

A young man in his twenties visiting his home town
Stopped by his childhood church to have a look around
The pastor was quit busy practicing his speech
The young man took a seat it'd been a while since he heard him preach

The pastor grabbed his bible and he shook it in the air
Listen what I tell you, the time is drawing near
The young man was very silent and stayed through the end
Then the pastor came right over to talk to his old friend

How has life been treating you? It's good to have you home
Your mother keeps us updated on all of the places you roam
How long will you be staying? Are you finished with your school?
I can get you a spot on the choir; you know I have a little pull

The young man looked right through the pastor as though he wasn't there
His face was heavy and dark. You could sense his deep despair
The answers aren't clear enough, I haven't found my way

I see the power in money then you tell me just to pray

What was it all for, you started in this room
The boiler three times broken and no needles in the broom
What makes you want to stay here? You are starving on the tithe
You fix the gates and mend the dogs and heartaches of all kinds

You hold the hands of those who live much nicer than you do
And even with all that they have, you drop all to see them through.
The preacher sat back firm and he looked around the room
His eyes were just as alive as a rose in full bloom

He ran and grabbed his pulpit and brought it to the boy
This is why I did it.   This is all of my joy
"That is just a junky board, grooved and splintered out"
"You are wrong" the preacher said. "This is what it is all about"

Your youth makes you self centered, so let's talk about just you
Your parents brought you to me.   When you were just brand new
Your eyes were barely open and they carried you in the door
As we sprinkled your dedication those waters touched this board

You had a terrible illness, when you were only five
The Dr's did not know if you would even survive
Your father carried you in, and laid you on the stage
The whole church touched your body and cried as we prayed

I remember when you graduated, months before the spring

The church prepared a celebration fit for a king
We paraded you down the aisle to show the Lord our work
And how another soldier had been prepared to change the world

The grooves that you point out, upon this ugly board
Were put here by my tears as payment to my Lord
You will see the sides of this board, are printed with my hands
From years of faithful preaching and hours of careful plans

I gave it all to God, many years ago
Those broken gates and wounded pups are seeds that I must sew
The boy said to the preacher, what good did it do
All of the work that you put into me and I stand here doubting you

Tears ran down the preachers face and a smile that would not end
"Ahh but where did you bring your doubts?" my child.   "Whose ear do you now bend"
This is where your home is.   No matter what you are paid
And those priceless grooves in my ratty old board were the difference that it made

A million jobs I could have had.   A million and one more
But none will ever pay as much as to see you walk back through that door……..Praise God!!!

[54]

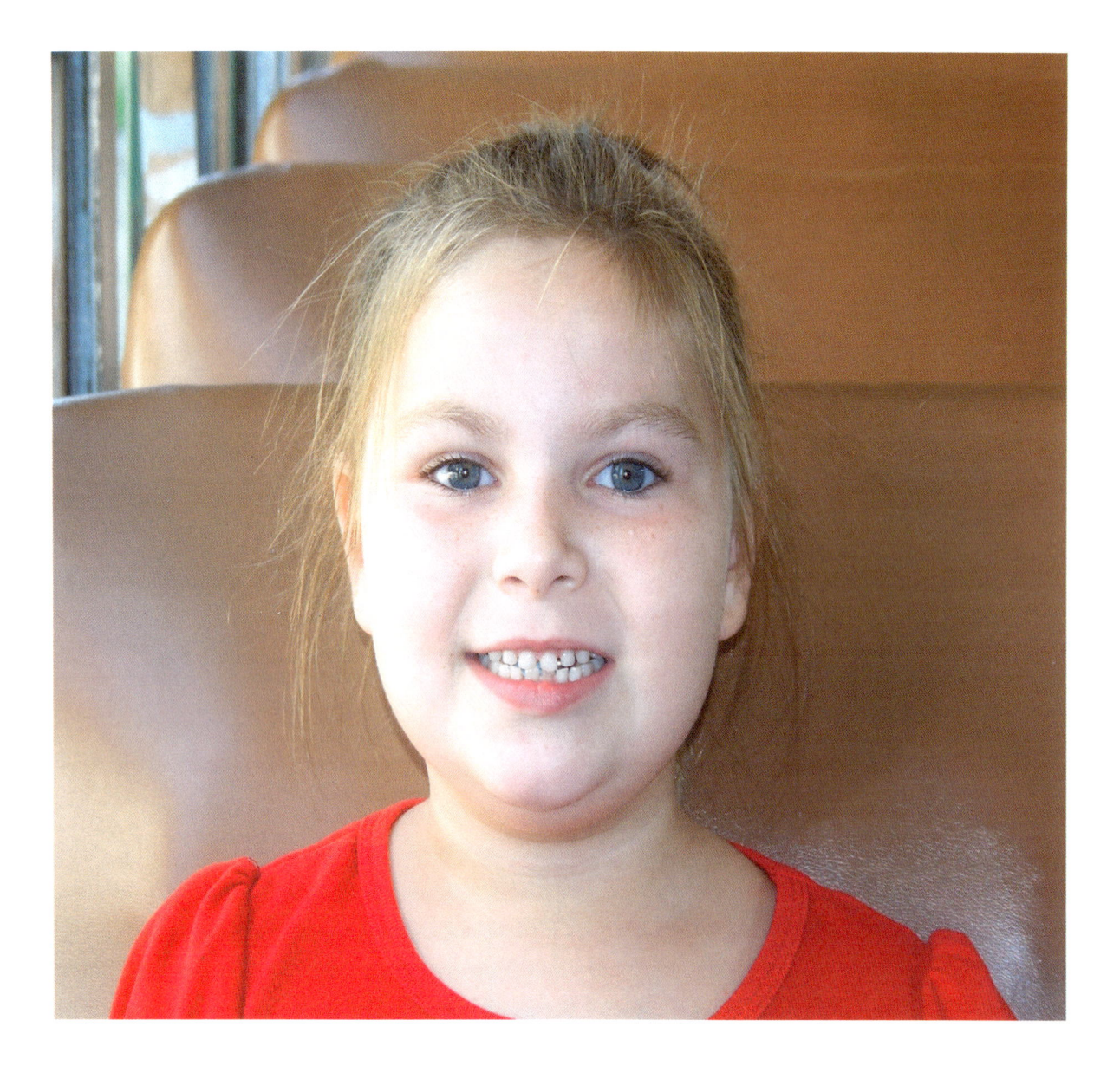

I think all people of religious conviction believe two things. The first is that there is a supreme being and the second is that there will come a time that all of this will end. How much preparation have you done? Are you ready?

## Listen to me children

Listen to me children
Take note of all your sin
Heed the desperate warnings
We are moving toward the end

The trumpets now are sounding
They are calling us to arms
Hold up your Holy Bibles
Denounce your worthless charms

Gods' people know what's happening
They are dancing in the street
They are ready for the journey
The homeland they shall meet

The Godless are showing worry
They are afraid of what they see
Their questions end in why
Their doubts are running free

His people have no questions
They have trained for many years
They know the answers given
They are shedding happy tears

For those who want to reach him
There is still a little time.
And those that have his truth inside
Will take you to Mt. Zion

Confess the sins that you carry
And accept God in your life
For He is coming back for us
By His words we must abide

The lights will shine from Heaven
A harp will play in tune
The arms of Heaven will extend for us
All others will meet their doom

If this is sounding scary
If this makes you afraid
Then you have got some work to do
And you had better start TODAY!!

Praise God!!

[56]

What do you do when you have a sin in your life that you know must be relinquished and you struggle with letting go?  The only answer, again and again, is to lay it at the feet of God and walk forward in victory.  Your fight can only be won through surrender.

## I GIVE UP

Lord I am giving up

I love and trust your way

But I am living in such sin

I am afraid to even pray


The vice that holds my heart

Is open for all to see

My weight is a constant reminder

That sin is still in me


I am open about my trials

I share that others may learn

But I cannot lead as a failure

Taking steps I haven't earned


I am baffled by my weakness Lord

I thought that healing had come

I prayed for strength through You Lord

I prayed that my struggles be done


I hear others who look upon me

Criticize and back away

They say that I am living in sin

As long as I weigh what I weigh


Lord with all respect

Am I in your light

Have I lost my salvation

Have I given up the fight

A voice came through the darkness

With a soft and gentle sigh

"Why do you question Me like this

Are you mocking My power in your life

I walked you through the fires of hell

And I saw that you made it through

Your worries are making you doubt now

And your doubts are destroying you

When you clean your house up fully

You pick one room to start

You clean it from top to bottom

And then move to another part

You can't do it all at once

And if you try, you will find

That nothing gets done but worry

And you will always be behind


Trust  Me now and don't lose hope

You have come so very far

Your healing is still in process

It is difficult reaching new stars


For souls who question your spirit

The point for them should be

When the urge is there to judge another

Just drop down to your knees

As a family we are bound

To hold each others dreams

Encouraging great success

Not allowing the Devils Schemes


Pat yourself on the back my child

And hold your head up high

Your walk with Me is not finished

I am preparing you to fly


So take your ears off of the gossip

Chase the sneers and the hatred away

Turn your eyes upon Jesus

And look full in His wonderful face


You can wear this as a burden

With your head hung to the ground

Or you can see it as the next challenge

On your journey to the Crown"


Thank you OH MY GRACIOUS GOD

My heart again is made whole

I allowed the judging to guide my feet

I allowed it to burden my soul


My worries I lay on your robe My Lord

Cleaning only the room that I'm in

For the healing only comes in Your time Lord

Not by my hand, my brothers or my friends………..Praise God!!

[63]

[64]

There is not much that I can say before this poem other than to say that if you are a person being abused or if you are asking your children to live in an abusive situation, the sooner that you get help, the better.  Wounds can heal but not until you stop the abuse.

## I KNOW YOU GIRL

There you are sitting with your eyes down at the floor
The same way that you have been 100 times before
So many try to help you but you smile and look away
The pain that plagues your heart seems to always be at bay

What could you have done that gives you such a guilt
What could be the reason that your prison walls were built
I see you look in awe at the children as they run
Someone should have taught you it's ok to have some fun

I know you, I know your pain, and I know your desperate cries
I know you like to hide away and I see your spirit die
I know that if I asked you, you would lie and say your fine
But I know you girl. Your hiding place is the same as mine

Will you ever open up and tell the world the truth
Will you know all bad things are not because of you
Will you hold your head up, even when you're wrong
And understand that crying sometimes can make you strong

Will you reach for help and believe there is a cure
Will you know that life is good when your heart is pure
Will you let him go and be able to stand upright

Never giving in or giving up the fight

There you are sitting with your eyes down at the floor
The same way that you have been 100 times before
So many try to help you but you smile and look away
The pain that plagues your heart seems to always be at Bay

I am sorry to you daughter, I did not realize
That every hit I took, you took with your eyes
Every angry word, that shot across the air
Was heard and digested and left you in despair

And now your mind is closed.   Your fear is trapped within
You don't know what play means or having close friends
Relationship is scary because anger is the boss
So you choose to sit alone, your heart is at a loss

And the more that you are lonely, the more you stay alone
The devil knows the tricks to pull to steal your happy home
He tells you that your pain, is all because of you.
And he dances when you are crying. Burying the truth

The only fight I am fighting, from now until I die
Is to undo all I have taught you, by keeping up this lie
My work will be to show you that you are not alone
God is holding you up from his precious holy throne

So put your eyes up to heaven child.   Don't cry another tear

Your pain will be forgotten when you let God have your fear
And Daddy's right about one thing.   In this the fault is mine
But hold your Mommy tight and we'll leave this pain behind

I will show you how to live, without a screaming fight
I will show you how to heal though it will take a while
I will show you how to pray, when you're weak and when you're strong
I will show you that you can be happy when all your fear is gone

It took awhile for me to see the troubles we were in
But now I know and I won't let that danger come back in
I hold you up to God my child.   And as we turn the page
The joy inside will be our strength through the rest of all of our days


Praise God!

Meredith

Hiding our sins away only helps them to grow. To truly heal from our sins we have to give it all up to God.

## HEALER BE THY NAME

I have a hidden cancer
I don't want you to see
It isn't what I want to show
Though it's a part of me

I carry it to work and home
I carry it to church
I keep it tucked far back inside
I make it stay submerged

I know that if you seen it
I know that if you knew
You'd keep your distance from me
You would leave me too

The pain it eats my joy up
It rests within my heart
I clean and clean it daily
But somehow it restarts

I am a crippled woman

Though my legs they work just fine
My faith is what keeps breaking
And the fault is strictly mine

I am giving all up to You Lord
I can carry it no more
And if I must be shunned by all
That's still better than before

I don't know where You'll take me
If I let You lead
But I know where I am going
Should I not concede

For You my heart I'll open
And let my fear subside
No longer will I hide my scars
Or keep my pain inside

I will sit down at Your table
And my manners I will use
I will dine with You my Father
For You shall make me new


And there will come a day
When someone wants to see
Exactly what I am made of

And what's inside of me

I want so bad to show them
That I am healed within
Held tightly in the arms of God
A Christian and a friend

I want the pain I've suffered
To help me learn to care
For others who are lost in life
And feeling that despair

I promise to be bold God
I will stand up straight and tall
For my Father who art in heaven
Will catch me should I fall

Please heal this poor old lady
Allow me one last chance
I want only just to serve You
And Your kingdom to advance

And let me start by saying
Thank You Oh My God
I turned from you again and again
And still You carried on

You stayed with me through battle

You stayed with me through rain
You held me though I looked away
You held me in my pain

I always want to serve You
And let the masses see
That my gift of healing came from God
In spite of doubts from me

He's all I need, He's all I need.   Jesus is all I need……….Praise

Everyone knows the story of the candy cane passed down from age to age.  Some say it is a tall tale and some say that it is true.  I say if we can give credit to the Lord then I am all for that!!

## My Shepherds Cane

It begins with a stick of pure white candy

Much like the beginning of our world

White for the virgin birth of our Savior

And for His sinless nature so pure


The candy is made rock hard

For the solid foundation in prayer

It is also the strength of the church

And our promise through God so fair


The shape is a J for the name of the Son

But is also is made for the hand

It is formed like the hook of the shepherd

For rescuing and guiding the lambs


The red on the cane is a tribute

Three small stripes to begin

One for each of the wounds

That Jesus endured for our sin


The last is the largest and greatest

For the blood there's a bold red stripe

That washed us for all of eternity

And promised eternal life


For God so loved the world

That His only son He gave

Not in order to condemn the world

But so that we might be saved

Enjoy your candy this season

And let the flavor stay

Remember that you have been spoken for

On this glorious Christmas Day……Praise God!!

When the flood came to Martinsville we were lucky. We lost water for about 10 days and power for a couple of days but we survived. So many homes were completely destroyed. Pictures and furniture and clothes and keepsakes that only come to you once in a lifetime were devoured by the rapid waters with not much warning.   The blessing in the flood was seeing the community work together like one big family and realizing that the only thing irreplaceable is our salvation.-----------------

## Martinsville on Solid Ground

The river runs the deepest yet
The dangers here much greater get
The shadows of our darkest hour
Nature showing us her power

Trembling, the masses roam
Nothing left to call a home
Walking through the milky mess
To dryer land and needed rest

All night the waters pressured in
Dams tried to hold but could not win
The final straw broke fully through
And sent hope down the river too

But just as swift as water came
The Lord pulled up the weak and lame
Where one was tired and one was lost
Another helped lift burdens off

Brother and brother bagging sand

Mothers leading family back to land
Children toted on shoulders and arms
Churches fell open to take in the swarms

The coast guard, police, and firemen too
Joined arms and forces as one large crew
The electric and gas and water were called
And stayed all night to restore us all

And in the midst of tragedy
The water flowing violently
The armor of the Lord intact
Our town stood as one and fought right back


Remember through the pain ahead
The truth is this, very simply said
On Christ the Solid Rock we stand
All other ground is sinking sand

ALL OTHER GROUND IS SINKING SAND…………..Praise God!!

[79]

[80]

The holiday of Thanksgiving is named Thanksgiving for a very good reason. We should be using that day to reflect and drink in the wonderful moments of family that are so few and far between in the changing world of today.

## Thanksgiving Feast

I loaded the van angry and tired
I wanted to stay home that day
A holiday for me is under the covers in bed
That is the American way

Instead I had to cook lots of food
And take off down the road
To share it with so many
That I barely even know

On the way to Grandma's house
The van began to choke
I had to pull it over
I thought, "This has to be a joke"

Could any other thing go wrong
To ruin this day for me
There was just one house to ask for help
I jumped out of the van to see

An elderly lady came to the door
I said "Can I use your phone?"
She let me in without delay

And I called to Grandmas home

I thanked the lady for helping me
And she asked me to stay inside
"I don't get many visitors this way"
So I sat with her for awhile

"I was just thanking God for my meal today
I would love to share it with you."
I was really worried about fixing my van
Though I was feeling hungry too

We said grace together and she smiled at me
"My daughter was just sixteen
When the Lord called her home to stay
She was so young and sweet

She used to love this holiday
We would invite in family and friends
And the house would fill with wonderful smells
She wished it would never end

I can close my eyes and see her dance
With the other girls there on the floor
Pretending to be ballerinas for us
And then dancing out of the door

We all would eat way too much
And then we hugged as each one left
My baby would ask to sit up on my lap
And I consoled her while she wept

As years went by her love of this day
Just grew like her locks of hair
She adored giving thanks to the Lord
And she loved having family there"

I felt a lump growing in my throat
As my new friend continued to speak
I suddenly remembered a time in life
When I too loved Thanksgiving week

Her table was bare except for some beans
Evidently straight from the can
I said "Wait right here, I have something to add"
And I got all of my food from the van

I brought rolls and stuffing and cranberry stuff
That I learned to make just last night
We dined like royalty until it was gone
And we talked about God in our lives

Then I heard a horn and I got up to see
My family had finally arrived
I went running to them with a smile and a hug
And I asked if my friend could ride

I wanted to take her to dinner with me
And share my family too
As she had shared her beautiful child
Which blessed me through and through

We went back inside only to find
That not a soul was there

No table no food and no telephone
Just torn curtains and a broken chair

I jumped in the van and there was my food
Still sealed and smelling warm
I tried to start the van again
As the key turned the engine roared

I followed my family to Grandma's house
Then unloaded the food and went in
I took special notice of the children playing
And the parents that were watching them

As they ate I just watched all the people smile
Someone noticed and asked me to eat
I am full I said.  As full as can be
Earlier today I had a wonderful feast

I jumped to my feet and raised my glass
"To all that sit here today:
Happy Thanksgiving I wish for you and your own
And may you never lose the meaning of this day"

Praise God and Happy Thanksgiving to you all!

[85]

[86]

Those of us that have been released from the pain of living our lives without God know the awesome and never-ending benefit to being in the family of God.  Having said that, we also have family and friends that choose to live their lives without God and struggle through the pain of existing without the power and light of the Lord to help them make it through.  There is such a desire to reach out to them and share with them but many times we are met with rejection.   It took me a long time to understand that it is my job to share, but not necessarily see it all the way through to the end.  Another man's victory will come only in God's time.  The best testimonies in life start with a seed that was planted years and years ago.

## KEEP HIM

I know that God will answer me

I know that He will speak

If only I come to Him and

Get down on my knees


My problems might seem tiny

Compared to all His woes

But I know that He will help

My voice is one He knows


And if the answer comes

And it's not the one I need

I will happily accept it

To the Lord I will concede

I have waited now for days

No answers have been sent

I pray to God each night and day

I pray and I repent

My friend who has no faith

Smugly calls to me

"Your God will not be answering you

There isn't one you see"

"If He is such a grand God

If He were there for you

Your answer would be given

Your troubles would be through"

"But still you sit here every night

And pray on bended knee

You cry out to a powerful God

That you can't even see"

"I 'm sad for you," my friend said

"I thought that you would learn

You're all alone in this world

Your riches you must earn"


You are right, I said,   about one thing

I have to pay my way

I work hard for my riches

And I worship and I pray


My God I see all around me

In the flowers and the trees

In the eyes of little children

In the waves upon the seas


They make my heart beat stronger

They lift me from my lows

I hear the sounds of life

And I forget my woes

"Your troubles are still present"

My friend lashed back at me

"For every day I see you

Down on bended knee"

"Your precious Lord forsook you

And left you here a shell

Crying for relief

From your unrelenting hell"

I have no such pain in my life

I am happy and content

I work hard for my Lord and

I happily repent

I want nothing more than to serve Him

And bring glory to His name

I am living for His purpose

I dare not bring Him shame

My friend looked very puzzled

He looked me in the eye

"Your great and powerful Lord" he said

"Has only been a lie"

"You spent your time alone in here

You asked Him for the truth

He gave you nothing but sore knees

Of that you have no use"

My answer just came, I told my friend

And much to my surprise

The Lord has shown great mercy

And now has made me wise

My prayers were for a friend of mine

Who fails to see the truth

He struggles with the meaning of life

He is lost and so confused

I have tried my best to help him out

And I am growing weak

My friend still fights against me

Every time he speaks

I had prayed to God to release me

From dealing with this one

I feel his soul is lost

He only wants to run

The Lord kept saying Keep Him

Your work is in My name

If he does not accept it

You are not to blame

I cried out to the Lord

I am growing tired

But all I heard was KEEP HIM

Save him from the fire

And now my friend you see the truth

The reason I'm not through

My pain is not because of God

My knees are sore for you

And if it takes eternity

To lift your soul up higher

Then that is what I pledge to God

To save you from the fire   …………..PRAISE GOD!!!

[94]

Doubts are the seeds of failure and should not be entertained.  If you have questions on your faith or your Christianity don't take it to your neighbor or your friend or your mentor.  Drop to your knees and take it to the Lord.  His is the only answer that will satisfy.  It is the only answer that is real.

## I WANT TO HEAR YOU SING

Walking down the path alone
I thought I knew the way
The path grew suddenly dark
I was alone and so afraid

I had walked a little too far
I didn't see the harm
I stayed a little too late
Now I must huddle to stay warm

I see a light on the path
My heart keeps drawing me near
But my head is telling me stop
And filling my mind with fear

I walk a little closer
To get a better look
My feet are heavy and slow

My confidence is shook

I see Your wonderful face Lord
I see Your tender eyes
But I really need Your hand Lord
To be sure this is no disguise

I want to see Your hands Lord
Your beauty, though it glows
Will not impress my doubts
And will not relax my woes

I have to see the holes Lord
The price You paid for me
The savior of unworthy souls
That no one else could be

I stand before You a child
Though my years are many and long
I feel new within Your sight
and together we wait on the dawn

Have I been all that you asked Lord
Have I walked a Christian walk
Have I helped to grow the family
And encouraged those who mock

A peace covered my heart and I heard:

Well done my child well done
You have been tried and true
Your name is in the book
And Heaven waits on you

Now play my precious baby
and let your laughter ring
your cares belong to me now
and I would like to hear you sing……… Praise God!

[98]

So many times we sit back and say nothing and share nothing because we are afraid that our talents are not strong enough.  God wants us to make a joyful noise unto him even if it is just noise.  All things in Praise are beautiful.   Don't be afraid to let God give birth to your talents and then use them to glorify His name.

## Born to fly

A caterpillar scooting slowly

I was lost without a care

My every day was full of nothing

There was misery and despair


My Master came and bound me tightly

A chrysalis became my home

It was a tight and warm protection

I was afraid and so alone


For days and nights, I hung there helpless

It seemed my life was surely through

The awesome weight of all of my burdens

Was wrapped up in the bondage too


The pain of changes began to wake me

The lack of sun within my tomb

The breathlessness at times alarmed me

It seemed to seal my coming doom


Then the Lord began to feed me

In my pain I thought to pray

He stopped me from my selfish crying

He told me to push the walls away


No common sense could I find in it

So I mocked and disobeyed

But through His faithful perseverance

My push began without delay

The sun came pouring into darkness

The light shone bright upon my face

The wind began to blow my body

As I broke my holding place

Then I looked out of my prison

And I gazed at all the world

Everything that I had known

Was different since my name was called

Again I heard my Lords direction

Still a greater plan unfurled

My mind was swimming in His grace

And I heard His precious voice

Fly my child, and touch the heavens

Take your wings and fly away

I have given you your freedom

And your soul has thus been saved


No fear I felt this time to follow

My God had ever been good to me

I took a jump straight up to heaven

And He was right, and I was FREE


My wings a gift from God eternal

I don't deserve this precious prize

My God forgave my misdirection's

It was ALWAYS His plan to see me fly

Praise God!!!

PRAISE HIS NAME!!

[104]

This poem is for my sister. My sister has been my best friend since I was born. She has been a great teacher to me about faith and hope.

## Dances on the wind

She closes her eyes and she sees an opening in the forest. A hole that to her is a door. The door will lead her to the destiny that calls out to her every day.

She moves through the opening and stretches with her arms as tall as she can reach, waking every muscle and feeling the sun bake on her golden brown skin.

She jumps into a tree and scales it with ease. She hangs from one limb and swings to another. She is a great climber and her heart dances on the wind.

She runs to the river and dives in head first. She holds her breath and swims under the water for a long stretch of river. When she rises she lifts out of the water like an angel drenched in heavens tears. She is a great swimmer and her heart dances on the wind.

She joins her tribe in dance and they praise the earth, the sun, the food, the health and the laughter that they all share. They dance until their feet are sore with blisters and her heart still dances on the wind.

Then a sudden noise shakes her conscious. Her eyes open and the forest is her room. Her skin is a pale alabaster from the lack of sun. Her two strong legs are really a wheelchair and her tribe is a clay village across the room on her dresser.

She is not a great warrior or a great climber or a great swimmer but her heart does dance on the wind........................ Praise God!!!

[106]

Sharing your darkest secrets and your deepest issues to others when guided by the Holy Spirit to do so may feel like the beginning of the end but it is really just the beginning………..

## Do as I ask…… The victory of confession.

You prayed to Him on bended knee and He told you what to do
You were afraid that the answer He gave was not the one for you

Your work is so important and your message must be clear
Remember when you teach we learn by sight and not by ear

He asked that you reveal yourself and you turned the other way
You were afraid of your enemy.   Afraid what some might say

But you walked in front of our church and you let your spirit soar
You showed to all the strength within when you opened up that door

You glowed just like a beacon, calling from the shore
Guiding in the helpless boats and lost they are no more

The beauty in that moment will never leave our minds
We saw you give it up to God and put your cares behind

That was just so perfect.   The way that we ALL grew
almost like it was planned by God…….unannounced to you-   Praise God!!!

[108]

Jesus loves the little children. All of the children of the world. Red, Yellow, Black, White, Fat, Thin, Burned, Broken, Beaten and Lost. Never be afraid to love a creation of God or to let yourself be counted as loveable.

## BLOOM WHERE YOU GROW

At the fair a girl was there, her wheelchair took much space

It held her arms and held her legs and it held her head in place

You looked at her and studied her and your eyes came back to me

Why was she making that awful noise Why did she not just speak

I was looking into your 5-year-old face and I chose my words with cause

How could I tell you and what could I say   My fear gave a very long pause

Your wisdom is what I will leave you with when my time on this earth is through

I want to answer your questions for you. I want you to know the truth

This child of God has a lot on her plate. Her work will be counted by our Lord

And though she may never speak a word, In heaven, her speech is adored

Every breath that goes in and thought that goes out is a precious and meaningful thing

She may never speak in words that you know but she can still make the angels sing

Life is quite difficult and our bodies can get in the way

The process that you must count on to is to learn, accept, and pray

Fight with your might to bloom where you grow and be strong in your faith as your walk

Your life spreads out seeds that will sew who you are and you don't really have to talk

Some people are asked to behold great pain and to march on ahead of the crowd

Some are just asked to do jobs mundane and continue to hold the fort down

Still others are asked to be speakers of truth and to call it all out to be shared

While some minister to only a few and giving the truth that they personally bear

Just do what you can, from where you are and don't be afraid to be bold

Don't wait for the world to hold you on high because your story will never get told

And when the light that your neighbor is holding appears to be growing dim

Hold them to God and help them because great lessons lie there within

You can't wait for miracles to walk through your life hoping God will remove all your pain

Take your pain on your walk and show God your strength. Be willing to walk in the rain

Some days you will drop to your knees from the pain and just pray that God keeps you in sight

Other days your anointing will lift your heart up and God will help you take flight

I barely could finish my sentence and I looked down to see your face

You had run to the girl confined to her chair at a frantic and hurried pace

You reached out to her and took her by hand. I saw her eyes get wide

You smiled to her with a glow and a nod and I watched your fears subside

Her noises stopped for just one moment, the air was thick with love

The connection between two Sisters of God was being watched from way up above

When you ran back to me and jumped in my arms it was clear for me to see

That your faith had just helped your flower to grow and your roots were setting you free

Praise God!!!

[112]

The church is such a blessing to us all but it can become a place of great pain when the people that God has trusted to spread the word become more interested in excluding those that don't measure up. It is so easy to forget that the church is there to bring in the weary and not push them out.

## WHO IS GOING TO HEAVEN

I proudly sit in obedience
Giving God the praise
I happily greet my church family
I rejoice through all my days

I think that I have reached the place
Where I am in the know
I think that I am heaven bound
I'm sure that I will go

I see a man walk briskly by
I can't believe my eyes
His clothes are tattered from age
and not the proper size

I do not lift to look at him
I will not say hello
how disrespectful can he be
He surely will not go

Another enters our church family
she holds her baby tight

There is no man to head her home
No father for the child

I will not lift to look at her
I will not say hello
for she has sinned against God's word
She will never go

The sermon is a long one
My neighbor is asleep
The pastor calls to all of us
to get up on our feet

My neighbor cannot hear him
I will not let him know
He is wasting time in church
He will never go

That night I had a dream
God came into my room
He shook his head in sorrow
He warned me of my doom

"I do not understand." I said
I never missed your word
I dressed for you respectfully
I listened and I heard

You did not listen carefully
you missed my whole intent
you ignore my children who need a hand
you ignore the one's I've sent

The man poorly dressed you wouldn't see
He will preach My sermons someday
I have heard his cries from the pits of hell
and I brought him home to pray

The young lady you passed by holding her child
her son will someday lead
He will learn through his mother the love of God
and that will plant a powerful seed

The man that you scorned leaning over in church
Asleep on the pew next to you
I worked hard to bring him into My house
His time is coming due

I made only one promise if he came through My door
I would fill his greatest request
He came through the door with an opened up heart
and the thing that he needed was rest

The one in our family that concerns Me the most
The one that I worry won't go
Is disrupting My home by judging My sheep

I won't allow that bitter seed to sew

Please hear Me now like never before
If you value your life in My light
Be found helping your family, not tearing them down
Or your soul will be lost in the fight

Praise God!!!!

[117]

[118]

The most amazing people in our lives are those that follow through with their testimony.  They minister to us both in their health and in their sickness and their word never loses significance because their witness only grows larger in the pain.  Pastor Leroy was an amazing man.  He and his wife brought me into the church by invitation and never ceased to fill my heart with glory in their witness.  When Pastor Leroy was torn with cancer and in the final stages of horrible pain he still cried and sang to the Lord on every clear moment.  He knew that he was going home and he was ready.  I cried uncontrollably at his funeral and a young woman asked me how I knew them.  I simply told her that he saved my life.  My life everlasting.  It is so important that we all understand the power that we have to witness to one another every day and remember what our purpose as Christians really is. Pastor is missed but his purpose lives on.

## PASTOR LEROY

Your smile is like a prayer itself

For deep inside it shows

That though the ocean rips and roars

Your garden of faith still grows


And through your pain you taught us all

To stand up straight and tall

And spite that Devil and his tricks

The Father heeds your call

You praise him in your greatest pain

With never one regret

You jump and clap and call his name

You know He paid your debt


I learned so much from you my pastor

My heart has begun to heal

I don't just fill the pew at church

My Christian faith is real


Our paths just crossed for one short hour

On one cool autumn night

My newborn child was in my arms

Her future yet defined


You reached for me and showed me God

You wanted me to see

And when my eyes were opened up

The spirit grew in me


I dance and shout with Victory

Praise God that you served Him

For your hand reaching out to me

Helped change me from within


My children have known God from the start

From the time that they were born

And because you shared His light with us

We will always serve the Lord


I know that you are growing weak

But only to this place

For soon you will see the brilliance of heaven

And your eyes will see His face

I laugh, I cry, I hold you up

I celebrate you today

With great assurance I tell you my friend

We will greet you in Heaven someday

PRAISE GOD!!!!

[123]

[124]

## I surrendered and He answered.

I don't deserve the kingdom but He promised it to me.
I was worthless. The world told me so. I did not count. I was not desirable or pretty or smart or wanted. I was no one.

In my pain I asked God why and He did not answer.
In my anger I yelled out to him and He did not answer.
In frustration I threw myself to the ground and begged and He did not answer.
I cried, I slept. I reconsidered.
Then I stood up in defeat and surrendered. Finally He answered.

He answered! Praise God!

He did not tell me how to be accepted by the world. That which was my original prayer. He told me to accept the world for what they are. He did not tell me how to be beautiful. He told me how to see my beauty for what it is. He did not teach me to count but rather how to stand up and be counted. He did not teach me to be desirable but rather how to desire His word first above all else.

Through all of these lessons I became smart and valuable. Through all of these lessons I became whole. Now I have been relieved of my pain, anger and frustration. I do still cry. I cry for the lost, I cry for the world, I cry for joy. I stand up now in Victory for when I surrendered to God He answered! Praise God!!!

[126]

## Painting outside of the lines

Meredith and Madailein were riding in the car. The sun was falling and it was so beautiful to see. The sun was a rich burnt orange and huge as it lowered down in the sky. There were clouds of dark blue and gray all around that were being ignited by the rays of the sun. It was pretty spectacular. I heard Madailein gasp at the clouds in the sky. She said "Look mom. God painted the sky again." Then Meredith said "Mom, God did not stay in the lines." I said." You are right honey. God did not stay in the lines. But doesn't that look nice."

The plan of the master does not always look or feel like what we would expect or even what we think we may want. It may not fit in the lines of what we think of as good or right but it is always the way that it should be if we are keeping the faith and walking with God. The path that He takes us on will not follow the lines made in the mind of man. God's path is greater than all and new in every saved soul. He is the sun burning hot through the sky guiding the dark clouds into the formation that will best achieve his Glory.

Lord, I pray that when you are reaching to change my course and I feel the burning of your convictions that I obey in an instant rather than trying to stay in the lines.

Praise God!

[128]

Remember with all love relationships, including that with our Lord and Savior, there are hardships and difficult times. Enjoy the good times but expect some bad too and support each other through the rain.

## My Love,

Roses are red when you show me your love

Roses are white for our peace from above

Roses are yellow for the friendship that we share

Roses are blue for our trials and despair

Roses are pink for the cute things that you

Roses are black for the hardships that we face

Roses are big for the wonders in life

Roses are small for the hard work and stife

I love you for all the roses

Every last stem in the bed

But I love you the most for knowing that all roses can't be red

Praise God!

[130]

When you find your life in Jesus Christ you no longer have to hold your head down and be miserable. You don't have to walk the earth pathetic and lost. Your debt is paid and your choices from that day come from a whole new place in life. A place of salvation and peace.

## PAID IN FULL

How precious is Your light

That shines upon my head

My world has just come crashing down

My innocence is dead

I hold to You, my knuckles white

My grip to not release

I bury my head deep in Your robe

So not to have to see

You stand for me without a word

Though blame is mine to bear

You let me rest my fears on You

You pay for me the fare
My debtors cannot pass You

They reach and fall away

Their power can't compare

To my shelter as I pray

I hear the storm and know it's there

I feel the waves of death

But even in the pits of Hell

Salvation's on my breath

My burdens that You lifted

Will drive me ever more

To work to please You justly

For still my heart is pure

Show me what to do Lord

Walk with me a spell

Let me host Your awesome light

And in Your kingdom

dwell…………Praise God!

[132]

A friend of mine from work had to let go of her father after having cared for him for a very long time in her home.  She was left with a void from the departure and I wrote this for her to help her let go.  I shared it with a friend from church shortly after that in the same situation and she and her husband found comfort in it as well.  The only blessing in the passing of someone in bad health is knowing that their body has been set free and they have found new legs of liberty with our Father in Heaven.

## Dad

You don't open the door anymore

You don't call my name anymore

You don't creak the floor anymore

Where will my mind take me

Where will my focus go

The Dr's appointments that I don't have to keep

The medicine that I don't have to dole

The symptoms that I don't have to record

Where will my mind take me

What will my watchful eye be spent on now

What will my better safe than sorry mind save

All of that work, all of that time, the inevitable has come to pass

The door has closed for good

The floor has settled

The voices have ceased

In my selfish mind I almost forgot that

The pain for you has stopped

The medicines for you have stopped

The confusion and depression for you has stopped

You are free

You are forever set free

Way to go Dad

Enjoy yourself

Carry with you that I love you still as I loved you always

Rest in peace

You held me on my first day and I held you on your last

God bless your soul and Goodbye……Praise God!!!

[135]

### *Praising Through*

As a little girl I saw a bible on the table of a family in my neighborhood. Their house was clean and tidy. They seemed happy and organized. I instantly felt warmth inside their home. I wanted to feel those things always.

I entered a church as a young woman. I saw the preacher work with his message. He preached and talked and sweat rolled down his forehead. Soon the sweat met with tears from his eyes. I could see that he believed in his message. I wanted to know what he knows.

Life gave me much heartache and many tears. Not tears of joy or revelation but tears of pain and desperation. So many choices and paths full of deceit and loneliness. So much hype and enticement leading me astray from what God would have me to be. I could not decide what path to take. Things were spinning out of control.

I found a love in the faces of my children. Each new birth brought a new expression, A new life A new curiosity. I found myself worrying if I was making right choices. I found myself regretting that they too would have to face the world and its paths. I could not rest for the fear that consumed me. Things were not at peace. No room for me to enjoy my gifts. It was then that my past came back to minister to me.

I heard you Lord, I remember the witness of the family in my childhood. I remember the calm on their hearts and their home. I remember that I wanted those things for myself as a child. I heard You through their happiness. I remember the peace

I heard you Lord, I remember the preacher in church. Living well on little because of his passion for the truth. The fire in his eyes as he shouted to us to heed the call. I heard You in his words and in his tears. I remember the Love

Now, I am trying to heal, from one of the worst tragedies that I have ever experienced. I feel like I am crawling on three limbs and not getting anywhere. I am in Your church; I have my home praise Your name at every turn. Where is my peace, where is the protection, why have you allowed this pain?

Would it make a difference for you to know, the Lord said to me, that the family who gave you witness buried three children before giving birth to five healthy ones. It was one of those children that became your friend and playmate and taught you songs of Christian love and redemption. And the preacher that you felt straight through to your bones, would it surprise you to know that he lost his wife and home in a fire and then made a life out of blaming Me before he pushed through his pain to redemption. Would it make you feel any less penalized to see that everyone is injured, broken, and lost? And it is not until they are broken that they rise. It is not until the eggshell of normalcy, that you fight so hard to protect, shatters that you can emerge into a new life with a new form preparing for the day that you will fly.

I know your pain has defeated you- but it has not defeated Me. Hold to Me more now than ever before and allow Me to hold you. And just as your tiny playmate became your first witness, and just as I brought you to the small church that blessed you as you witnessed the power of a brutal fire now concealed in the words and eyes of a man born again. You too will give witness.   And just as you were searching, so will others be.    And just as you were blessed, others will be blessed by you and just as you found the strength to carry on, they will find strength as well.

Thank You Lord.  My lesson learned.  I praise You and I share this with message with all….

Be bold in your joy, MORE bold in your pain

Be bold in your sun, MORE bold in your rain


Be bold when you know, MORE bold when you don't

Be bold when you pray, MORE bold for those who won't

Expect to be fed, in pain and in praise

Expect to be led, for all of your days

 Sometimes walking slowly, sometimes running fast

Sometimes barely crawling, Sometimes finishing last

 Praise God through your struggles, Take Him with you as you go

Let the world see you lifted, through His never ending glow

PRAISE GOD!!

[138]

The next two poems are about these little people that God brought to my life. The little ones that could not eat or drink when they came to me but now they feed my soul every day.

Through all of my mountains and deserts and tears and happiness, these two children of God were a force full of Gods light and truth.

MEREDITH "BABY GIRL" WALKER

[140]

She is the first breath in the morning

The shine of the sun on the lake

The dew dripping off of a blade of grass

The icing on the cake

She's a sunbeam escaping a cloud front

Sending light to the ground beneath

She's the sunset as orange as fire

As it disappears into the reef

She is iced tea under a tall tree

Smelling honeysuckle in the air

She is a whole day just for swimming

And cotton candy at the fair

She is a puppy on Christmas morning

That has found a lifelong friend

She is everything in life that is fine

The beginning, duration and end…….Praise God!!

Madailein "KiKi" Walker

It occurred to me this morning

As I dressed you for your school

You are my little sunshine

You are my precious jewel


I named you for your eyes that glow

My bright and shining one

Who knew that you were born from it?

Who knew you lit the sun


A warm and inviting sunbeam

That lights all in its path

One glance from your blue eyes

And the flowers begin to dance


The birds welcome you every morning

With a song they sing in praise

The Trees are full and healthy

Because they are drinking in your rays

The breeze tries to cool you down

But never will it win

Because the fire that you capture

Is coming from within


It's hard to look straight at you

For the eyes are overwhelmed

Your power is exuded

The whole world is your realm


You warm me when we are together

And your absence leaves me cold

Your beauty is a timeless joy that

Cannot be bought or sold……Praise God!!

[145]

[146]

Sunday School is an extension of your praise and worship.  When you have a class that is on fire for the Lord it is worth more than you can imagine.  My Sunday school teacher prepares a lesson every Sunday but we rarely get to the lesson.  We get very much caught up in the praise and prayer request part of class and sometimes just can't move past the praise!!

## JOY IN CLASS

Walking into church this morn
I wished I had stayed home
My heart was heavy with my woes
My thoughts wouldn't leave me alone

I was filled with anger, confusion and stress
I was not in the right frame of mind
If the lord had looked in my heart right then
What a terrible mess he would find

A friend of mine smiled at me
I shot back a hearty smile
Though I wished I could have disappeared
To deal with the pain inside

I sat in the back of the Joy Class and hid
I did not want to participate
I just wanted it to be over quick
So I hung my head in wait

Steve opened up the class
With a story of his praise
Tears rolled down his cheeks
With the words he had to say

Then another testified
His week had been so rough
He just wanted to thank the Lord
For making him so tough

A lady in the front row
Held her hand up high
"Thank the Lord" she called out
And tears were in her eyes

"The Lord stayed with me this week
I could never have made it through
He walked with me and talked with me
And I wanted to share it with you"

My heart began to loosen
As I listened to her speak

I felt my body relaxing
My spirit started to peak

I looked up from my misery
My family all around
My problems had been heavy
But I laid them on the ground

I got up from my chair
And headed for the door
And left my problems laying there
Dying on the floor

I shouted to God "I'm Sorry
I did not let You lead
I tried to hide my problems
I was blind but now I see"

"But You Did Listen" God Said
"When I saw your fear not pass
I walked you into to church today
And put you in Joy Class

You fought me as you showered
You fought me while you dressed
You did not want to come to church
But you knew that it was best

Church is not for Saint hood
Church is where you learn
To heal your open wounds
And get rid of your concerns

The MOST important time
To be within the church
Is when your pain starts hiding
The message in my words

Thank you Oh My God
Your Mercy is divine
I won't forget this healing
And the answers you helped me find

You are welcome child
Be strong in all you do
Do not forget my message
It always will be true

And share this with your family
Next week when class resumes
For another will be hiding
And their healing comes through you…….PRAISE GOD!!!

[151]

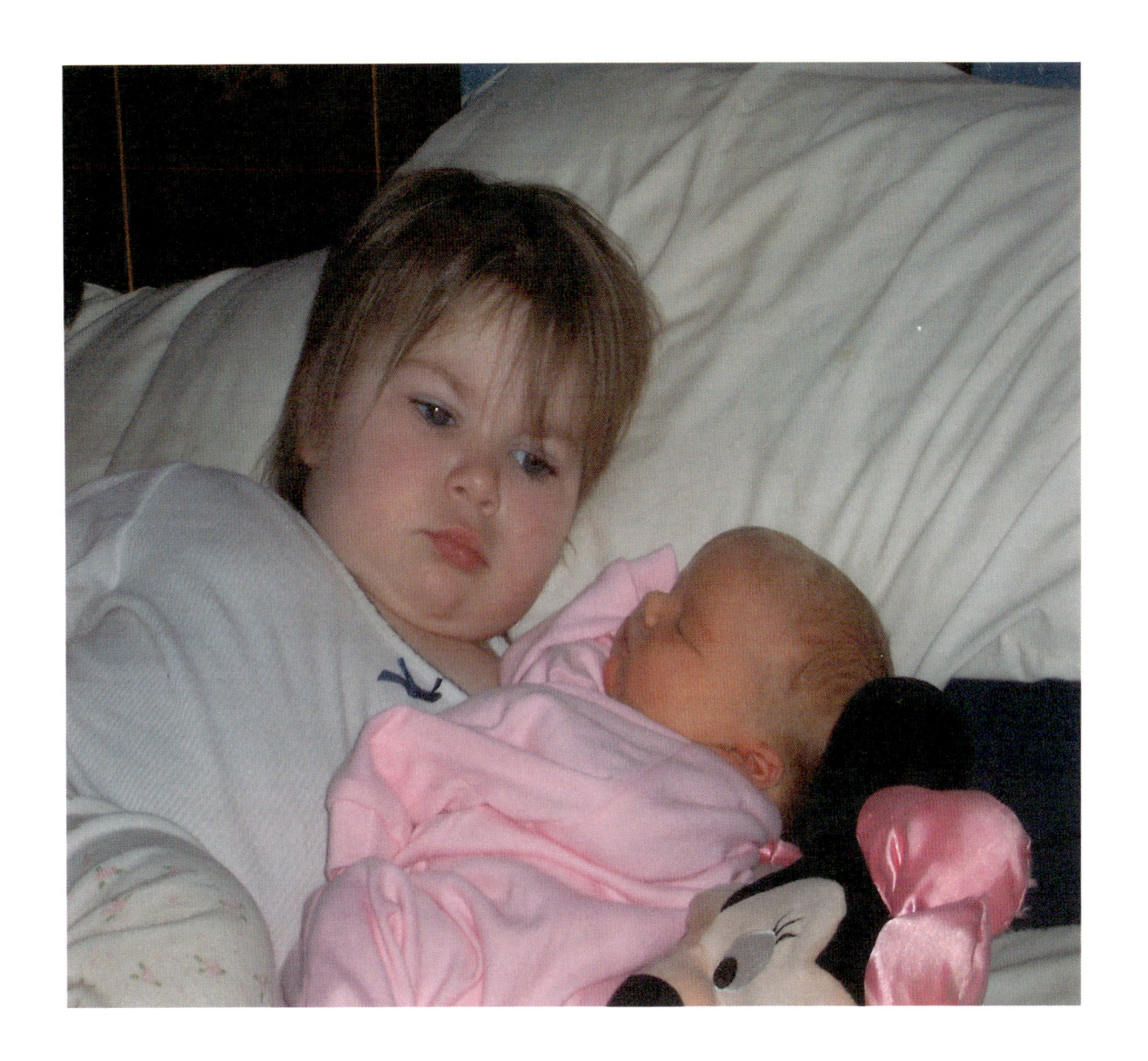

[152]

I left this for last poem for last.  It is the walk that continues.  Out in faith.  Leaving behind my baggage and my fears and reaching for tomorrow with curious and open arms.  Never ever forgetting to PRAISE GOD!!

## **OUT IN FAITH**

My feet are heavy and dragging Lord
as I walk along this road
Others seem to breeze on by
With a much much lighter load

My heart hurts Lord and I won't lie
I want to breeze by too
My feet just feel so heavy Lord
Can I confide in you

I feel some guilt from times ago
Some choices that I made
That caused the pain that others felt
Some games that I chose to play

I hold them close to hide them Lord
So no one else can see
They are not things that I am proud of Lord
Not what is expected from me

I feel the hurt from yesterdays Lord
Moments that did not go well
My heart just sighs to think of them Lord

Too much to ever tell

I feel the pain of anger Lord
For things that I did not choose
And regrets by the bucket full
From wishes left unused

But the biggest bag that I carry
Is the one that holds my dreams
It's the heaviest bag that I have Lord
Unopened it would seem

Lord my baggage just drags me down
It is so hard for me to move on
I carry it with me in my waking hours
Then I hold it from dusk until dawn

I know that you want me to let go Lord
I see Your hands reaching for me
But with all of my baggage and problems Lord
How could I ever be free

I will step out in faith today Lord
I will not stand and wait to be passed
Though my feet are still heavy today Lord
Someday they will be light and be fast

I promise not to look back Lord
At my baggage that I laid on the ground
I don't care what becomes of that mess
For, through You, I am no longer bound

As I look up I can see my dreams Lord
Did You open that bag for me
The other bags just disappeared
And my dreams are now ALL that I see

I am walking in faith with You Lord
Holding my Bible and free from my bags
I am learning to breeze by delivered and free
Wearing my crown in place of my rags

I GIVE ALL GLORY AND PRAISE TO ALMIGHTY GOD!!

**There is no end to the story with Jesus…..**

In all that you have read in these pages, I hope that you can feel my victory and peace in Jesus. The things that have hurt me the most have no power over the person that I am today. My life moves forward one step at a time through my Lord and Savior. I had so many hurts and so many regrets until the Lord saved me. Now I have so many hopes and so many dreams. I have been judged and been guilty of judging, I have been hurt and been guilty of hurting, and I have been lost and been guilty of losing my focus in the face of fear. Through it all, I have learned that the only answer is God. Keeping my faith in the darkest of hours is in itself the victory. All praise for all lessons be to God for life everlasting and peace on earth. God is good all the time, through all things, forever.

A young man giving testimony after a long bout with drug addiction said in giving witness to his salvation that the only being powerful enough to keep God out of our lives is ourselves. Choose God today and every day. Life is not easy for anyone. No matter what you believe, you will have struggles and you will face tragedy. To face it all alone is a tragedy in itself when God is there waiting for you to call. Waiting to be that hand to hold. Waiting to fill your heart with peace and remove your fear. I hope that you are reading this knowing that God is real. If you are not, I hope that you will let something that you read here plant that seed. I can tell you from experience that it is never too late. It is so easy. Just Praise God, Praise God, Praise God and then, when all else fails, Praise God!!!

**Believe and give praise with all of your heart and you will find peace in your life, _especially_ in the valley. PRAISE GOD!!!**

You can send comments through Poeticpraise13@yahoo.com

[158]

[159]

3951385

Made in the USA